PLANETS
JUPITER

ABDO
Publishing Company

A Buddy Book by Fran Howard

VISIT US AT

www.abdopublishing.com

Published by ABDO Publishing Company, 8000 West 78th Street, Edina, Minnesota 55439.

Printed in the United States.

Editor: Sarah Tieck
Contributing Editor: Michael P. Goecke
Graphic Design: Maria Hosley
Cover Image(s): Photodisc.
Interior Images: Library of Congress (page 22); Lushpix (page 28); NASA: Ames Research Center (page 25, 27), Jet Propulsion Laboratory (page 6–7, 11, 12, 13, 23, 29, 30), Johnson Space Center (page 26), Photos.com (page 9, 15, 17).

Library of Congress Cataloging-in-Publication Data

Howard, Fran, 1953-
  Jupiter / Fran Howard.
      p. cm. -- (The planets)
  Includes index.
  ISBN 978-1-59928-827-7
  1. Jupiter (Planet)--Juvenile literature. I. Title.

QB661.H69 2008
523.45--dc22
                                2007014755

Table Of Contents

The Planet Jupiter

Jupiter is a planet. A planet is a large body in space.

Planets travel around stars. The path a planet travels is its orbit. When the planet circles a star, it is orbiting the star.

The sun is a star. Jupiter orbits the sun. The sun's **gravity** holds Jupiter in place as it circles.

It takes Jupiter about 12 Earth years to orbit the sun. That means one year on Jupiter is 12 times as long as a year on Earth.

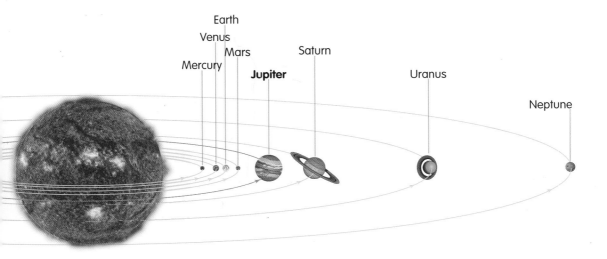

Mercury
Venus
Earth
Mars
Jupiter
Saturn
Uranus
Neptune

There are eight planets orbiting our sun. Each planet has its own orbital path. And, each planet takes a different amount of time to travel completely around the sun.

Our Solar System

OUTER PLANETS

Neptune

Uranus

Saturn

Jupiter

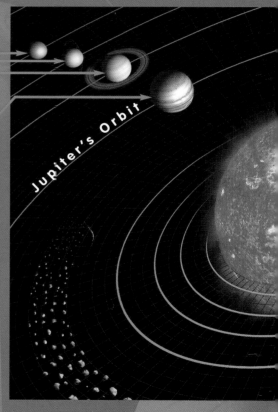

Jupiter's Orbit

Jupiter is one of eight planets that orbit our sun. The planets orbiting the sun make up our solar system.

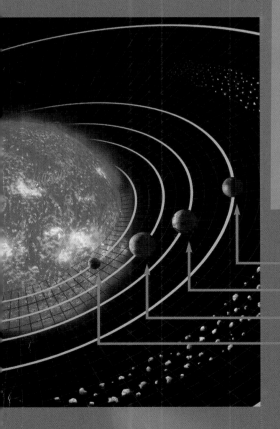

The other planets in our solar system are Mercury, Venus, Earth, Mars, Saturn, Uranus, and Neptune.

Jupiter is about 484 million miles (779 million km) from the sun. It is the fifth-closest planet to the sun.

Mars

Earth

Venus

Mercury

INNER PLANETS

The Stormy Planet

Jupiter is known for having many strong storms. These storms occur everywhere. There is powerful lightning. And, winds reach speeds of 220 miles (350 km) per hour.

Jupiter's Great Red Spot is one giant storm. This storm has lasted for more than 300 years!

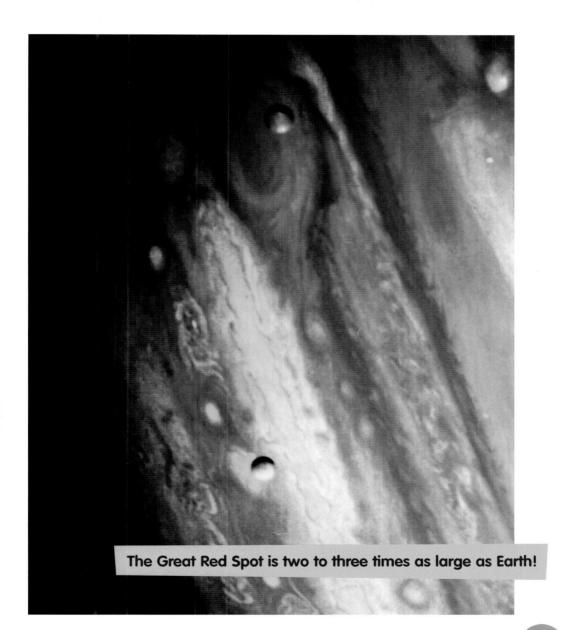

The Great Red Spot is two to three times as large as Earth!

A Closer Look

Jupiter is the biggest planet in our solar system. Orange and brown clouds cover the planet.

Jupiter has a ring system. This system has three parts. These are the halo, the main ring, and two gossamer rings. Jupiter's **gravity** holds the rings in place. Scientists think these rings are made of dust from some of Jupiter's moons.

Gossamer Rings

Main Ring

Halo

Amalthea

Adrastea

Metis

Thebe

Jupiter's moons create divisions between the rings using gravity. Scientists call these moons "shepherd satellites".

There are at least 63 moons in Jupiter's sky. Four of Jupiter's moons are very large. These are named Europa, Callisto, Ganymede, and Io.

Ganymede and Callisto are as big or bigger than the planet Mercury! Some scientists think Jupiter's moon Europa has a liquid ocean. This ocean is covered in ice.

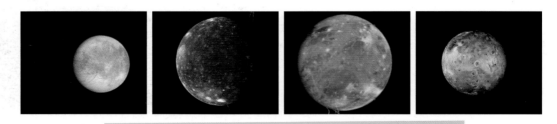

Jupiter's four largest moons *(from left to right)* are Europa, Callisto, Ganymede, and Io.

The *Cassini* spacecraft captured this
shot of Io in front of Jupiter's clouds.

What Is It Like There?

Layers of gases surround each planet. These layers are a planet's **atmosphere**. The atmosphere on Jupiter is mostly made of **hydrogen**. The atmosphere is also part **helium**.

Planets spin on an **axis**. This spinning creates night and day.

Jupiter spins faster than any other planet. It makes one complete spin in about 10 hours. So, a day on Jupiter is less than half the length of a day on Earth.

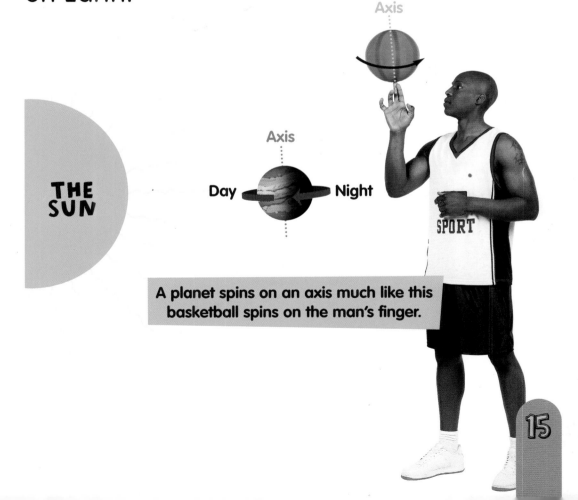

THE SUN

Axis

Axis

Day

Night

A planet spins on an axis much like this basketball spins on the man's finger.

SPORT

15

Jupiter makes about as much heat as it gets from the sun. At one time, Jupiter was twice as large and much hotter than it is now!

Some scientists say Jupiter has a thin layer of water clouds. Lightning occurs in these clouds.

Jupiter's lightning can be 1,000 times as powerful as the lightning on Earth!

A Gas Giant

Scientists think Jupiter may have a rocky core. But, it does not have a surface to stand on.

This is because Jupiter is a gas giant. Gas giants are mostly made of gas. Saturn, Uranus, and Neptune are also gas giants.

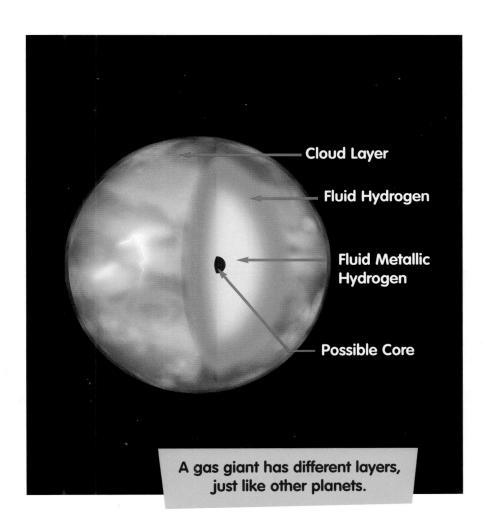

Cloud Layer

Fluid Hydrogen

Fluid Metallic
Hydrogen

Possible Core

A gas giant has different layers,
just like other planets.

Discovering Jupiter

No one knows who discovered Jupiter. But, it is visible in Earth's night sky. So, people have known about Jupiter for a long time.

The Romans named Jupiter after the ruler of their gods.

The Roman god Jupiter.

Galileo was very interested in studying the night sky. He discovered many things about our solar system.

Italian astronomer Galileo discovered Jupiter's four large moons in 1610. That was about 400 years ago! It is believed that this was the first time anyone saw a moon other than Earth's moon.

Scientists first saw Jupiter's Great Red Spot in 1664 or 1665.

The Great Red Spot isn't always red.

Missions To Jupiter

Scientists began sending **spacecraft** to Jupiter in 1972. During these **missions**, the spacecraft did flybys. This means the spacecraft passed by the planet instead of stopping or orbiting.

The *Pioneer* spacecraft flybys took place in 1973 and 1974. In 1979, *Voyager I* and *II* discovered Jupiter's rings.

The *Pioneer* missions took the first images of Jupiter's atmosphere. They also took images of some of Jupiter's moons.

The *Galileo* **spacecraft** left Earth in 1989. It dropped a **probe** into Jupiter's gas layers to learn more about them.

Galileo's **mission** lasted 14 years. In 2003, scientists crashed *Galileo* into Jupiter. They did this so it wouldn't hit one of Jupiter's moons.

In 2000, the *Cassini-Huygens* probe flew by Jupiter. On its way to Saturn, it took images of Jupiter.

Galileo traveled near Jupiter's moon Io.

The probe from *Galileo* helped scientists understand more about Jupiter's clouds.

Fact Trek

Using a telescope, you can see Jupiter's Great Red Spot from Earth. Over time, the Great Red Spot has changed color from orange to dark brown.

The symbol for Jupiter is a **hieroglyphic** drawing of an eagle. This is for the Roman god Jupiter's bird.

Jupiter is the largest of the eight planets in our solar system. So, some people call Jupiter "The Big One."

Jupiter is known as "the solar system's vacuum cleaner." This is because it's strong gravity pulls space objects toward it. More space objects hit Jupiter than any other planet!

Voyage To Tomorrow

People are continuing to explore space. They want to learn more about Jupiter.

A space **probe** called *New Horizons* did a flyby in February 2007. During its **mission**, it studied Jupiter's moons.

NASA plans to launch *Juno* in 2011. *Juno* will orbit Jupiter, too.

Space probes help scientists learn about planets.

Important Words

atmosphere the layer of gases that surrounds a planet.

axis an imaginary line through a planet. Planets spin around this line.

gravity the force that draws things toward a planet and prevents them from floating away. Stars use this force to keep planets in their orbit.

helium a light, colorless gas. Helium is used in balloons to make them float.

hieroglyphics a system of writing that uses pictures to represent ideas and sounds.

hydrogen a colorless gas that burns easily and is lighter than air. When hydrogen is mixed with oxygen, it forms water.

mission the sending of spacecraft to perform specific jobs.

NASA National Aeronautics and Space Administration.

probe a spacecraft that attempts to gather information.

spacecraft a vehicle that travels in space.

Web Sites

To learn more about **Jupiter**, visit ABDO Publishing Company on the World Wide Web. Web sites about **Jupiter** are featured on our Book Links page. These links are routinely monitored and updated to provide the most current information available.

www.abdopublishing.com

INDEX